Hallo, ich bin Anoki!
Für jede Seite, die du fertig hast,
malst du eine Wolke aus.

2 3

4 5 6 7 8

9 10 11 12 13 14 15 16 17

18 19 20 21 22 23 24 25 26

27 28 29 30 31 32 33 34 35

36 37 38 39 40 41 42/43

▶ Link.
Verbinde.

chair	teacher	picture	board	table
Stuhl	Lehrerin	Bild	Tafel	Tisch

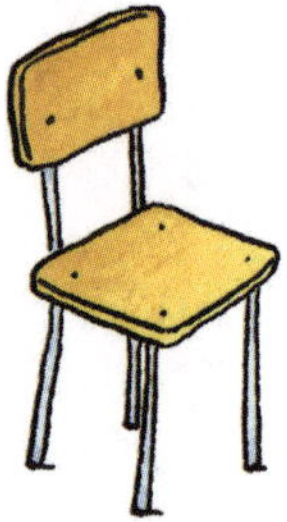

► **Write in and copy.**
Spure nach und schreibe ab.

Es gibt zwei Artikel:
a – ein oder eine
the – der, die oder das.

 a board	
 a chair	
 a picture	
 a table	
 the teacher	

School

3

▶ True ☑ or false ☒? Tick.
Kreuze an: wahr ☑ oder falsch ☒?

Das ist ein Tisch. –
It's a table.

 It's a table. ☑

 It's a teacher. ☐

 It's a table. ☒

 It's a board. ☐

 It's a board. ☐

 It's a chair. ☐

 It's a teacher. ☐

 It's a picture. ☐

 It's a picture. ☐

 It's a chair. ☐

School

4

► Read and tick.
Lies und kreuze an.

Lies auch einmal laut.

	Hello!	
	Goodbye!	
	Can you help me?	
	Hello!	
	Goodbye!	
	Can you help me?	
	Hello!	
	Goodbye!	
	Can you help me?	

School

▶ Link.
Verbinde.

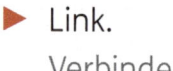

School uniform

jacket	shirt	skirt	pullover	trousers
Jacke	Hemd	Rock	Pullover	Hose

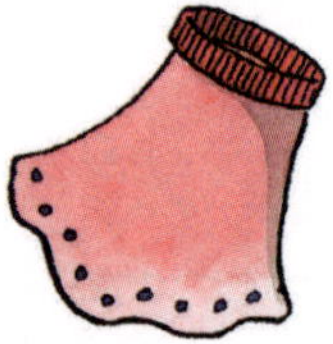

▶ Write in and copy.

Spure nach und schreibe ab.

Ohne Artikel, dafür mit Plural-s: trousers – eine Hose.

	a jacket	
	a pullover	
	a shirt	
	a skirt	
	trousers	

7

▶ Read and write.
Lies und schreibe.

one	two	three	four	five
1	__	**3**	__	**5**

eleven	twelve	thirteen	fourteen	fifteen
11	**12**	__**3**	**1**__	**15**

six	seven	eight	nine	ten
6	__	**8**	__	___

sixteen	seventeen	eighteen	nineteen
1__	**1**__	_____	_____

twenty
2___

▶ Count and colour in.

Zähle und male aus.

Das ist eine Raupe. –
It's a caterpillar.

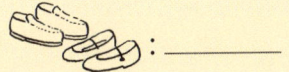 : _____

9

▶ Link.
Verbinde.

football	reading	skateboarding	swimming	music
Fußball	lesen	Skateboard fahren	schwimmen	Musik

▶ Find and write in.

Spure die Wörter nach.

reading

music

football

swimming

skateboarding

a	e	t	z	**r**	**e**	**a**	**d**	**i**	**n**	**g**	h	r
s	w	i	m	m	i	n	g	h	j	e	b	v
b	e	a	n	i	f	o	o	t	b	a	l	l
s	k	a	t	e	b	o	a	r	d	i	n	g
x	b	s	h	m	u	s	i	c	d	n	p	b

▶ True ☑ or false ☒? Tick.
Kreuze an: wahr ☑ oder falsch ☒?

 I like music. ☑

 I like music. ☒

 I like reading. ☐

 I like football. ☐

 I like reading. ☐

 I like skateboarding. ☐

 I like football. ☐

 I like swimming. ☐

 I like swimming. ☐

 I like skateboarding. ☐

Hobbies

☐ 12

▶ **Which hobbies do you like? Read and tick.**
Welche Hobbys magst du? Lies und kreuze an.

Lies immer Frage und Antwort:
Do you like music? –
Yes, I do. / No, I don't.

	Yes, I do. ❤️	No, I don't. 👎
Do you like skateboarding?		
Do you like music?		
Do you like reading?		
Do you like swimming?		
Do you like football?		

13

▶ **Read, link and write in.**
Lies, verbinde und spure nach.

Hobbies

My hobby is swimming.

My hobby is reading.

My hobby is skateboarding.

▶ **Read and colour in.**
Lies und male aus.

Hobbies

> *playing – so viele Hobbys gibt es mit diesem Wort!*

I like playing ...

| football |

| tennis |

| the guitar |

| games |

| in the park |

| on the computer |

15

Rooms

▶ Link.
Verbinde.

living room	bedroom	bathroom	kitchen	garden
Wohnzimmer	Schlafzimmer	Bad	Küche	Garten

► Link.
Verbinde.

lamp	shelf	table	chair	bed
Lampe	Regal	Tisch	Stuhl	Bett

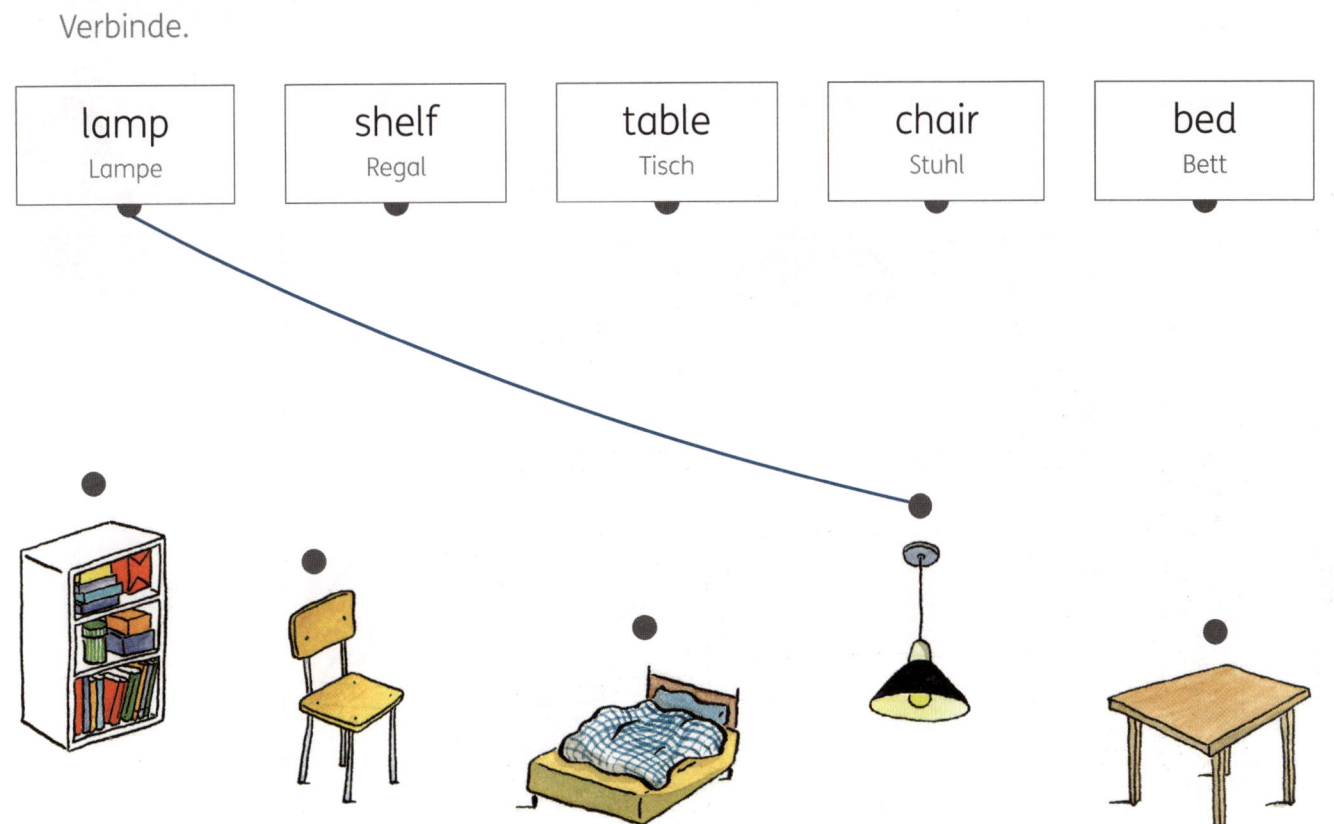

▶ **Read and colour in.**
Lies und male aus.

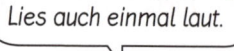
Lies auch einmal laut.

My bedroom

There is a green lamp, a ...

lamp

shelf

bed

chair

table

□ 18

▶ **Read, tick and draw.**
Lies, kreuze an und male.

Wie mein Zimmer wohl aussieht?

Anoki's bedroom

☐ bed ☐ lamp ☐ shelf ☐ chair ☐ table ☐ sofa ☐ picture

▶ Link.
Verbinde.

evening	afternoon	morning	night
Abend	Nachmittag	Morgen	Nacht

Time

20

▶ Find and write in.

Spure die Wörter nach.

Achte auf die kleinen Wörter:
in the morning – am Morgen
at night – in der Nacht.

in the morning   in the afternoon   in the evening   at night

w	e	r	z	s	r	a	t		n	i	g	h	t	m	k
i	n		t	h	e		a	f	t	e	r	n	o	o	n
m	l	h	o	f	w	d	u	i	o	m	t	r	m	v	d
j	i	n		t	h	e		e	v	e	n	i	n	g	m
b	e	r	n	s	u	b	n	d	s	u	y	m	c	l	e
v	g	**i**	**n**		t	h	e		m	o	r	n	i	n	g
z	b	s	u	o	e	s	e	t	d	n	p	h	l	i	a

Time

21

► True ☑ or false ⊠? Tick.
Kreuze an: wahr ☑ oder falsch ⊠?

Wie spät ist es – What time is it?

 It's 2 o'clock. ☑

 It's 5 o'clock. ☐

 It's 2 o'clock. ⊠

 It's 11 o'clock. ☐

 It's 11 o'clock. ☐

 It's 5 o'clock. ☐

 It's 7 o'clock. ☐

 It's 7 o'clock. ☐

☐ 22

▶ **Read and link.**
Lies und verbinde.

Lies auch einmal laut.

 In the morning

 In the afternoon

In the evening

 At night

I sleep.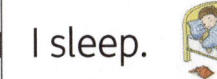

I eat.

I go to school.

I play.

Time

► Link.
Verbinde.

spring	winter	summer	autumn
Frühling	Winter	Sommer	Herbst

Year

► Write in and copy.

Spure nach und schreibe ab.

Das Jahr beginnt im Frühling –
The year starts in spring.

in spring	
in summer	
in autumn	
in winter	

Year

► Read and link.
Lies und verbinde.

Lies auch einmal laut.

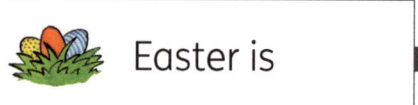 Easter is

 in autumn.

 Christmas is

 in winter.

 Halloween is

 in summer.

 My birthday is

 in spring.

Year

▶ Read and write.
Lies und schreibe.

Viele Monate sind fast gleich: December – Dezember, May – Mai.

autumn   spring   summer   winter

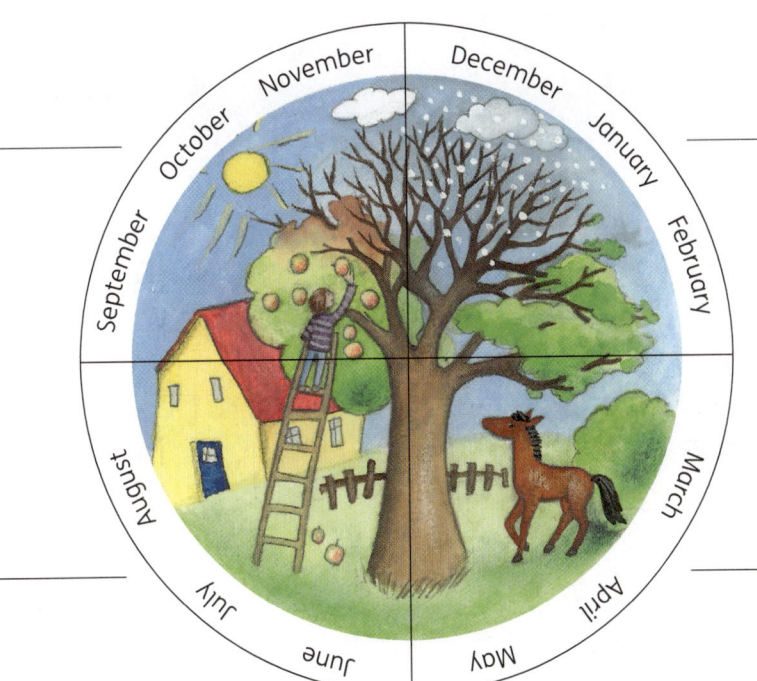

Year

▶ Link.
Verbinde.

sunny	cold	windy	cloudy	hot	rainy
sonnig	kalt	windig	wolkig	heiß	regnerisch

28

▶ True ☑ or false ☒? Tick.
Kreuze an: wahr ☑ oder falsch ☒?

Wie ist das Wetter heute? – What's the weather like today?

 Today it's hot. ☑

 Today it's windy. ☐

 Today it's hot. ☒

 Today it's rainy. ☐

 Today it's cloudy. ☐

 Today it's cold. ☐

 Today it's windy. ☐

 Today it's cloudy. ☐

 Today it's cold. ☐

 Today it's rainy. ☐

Weather

29

▶ Read and write.

Lies und schreibe.

____ hot
heiß

____ shorts
kurze Hose

____ sandals
Sandalen

4 sunglasses
Sonnenbrille

____ eat ice cream
Eis essen

____ swim
schwimmen

Summer

30

▶ How old are you? Colour in.
Wie alt bist du? Male aus.

Weißt du auch,
wie alt ich bin?

I'm __ years old.

► Link.
Verbinde.

banana	cucumber	strawberry	apple	tomato
Banane	Gurke	Erdbeere	Apfel	Tomate

32

► Find and write in.
Spure die Wörter nach.

banana    strawberry   apple   tomato   cucumber

a	e	s	t	r	a	w	b	e	r	r	y	r
h	w	a	m	c	u	c	u	m	b	e	r	v
b	e	a	p	p	l	e	o	t	b	a	v	l
s	**b**	**a**	**n**	**a**	**n**	**a**	v	r	i	h	n	g
x	b	t	o	m	a	t	o	c	d	n	p	b

▶ Write and colour in.

Schreibe und male aus.

Wieviel kostet es? –
How much is it?

banana	tomato	apple	cucumber	strawberry
It's £ __2__.	It's £ ____.	It's £ ____.	It's £ ____.	It's £ ____.

► What do you like? Read and tick.
Was magst du? Lies und kreuze an.

Lies immer Frage und Antwort:
Do you like apples? –
Yes, I do. / No, I don't.

	Yes, I do. ♥	No, I don't. 👎
Do you like apples?		
Do you like tomatoes?		
Do you like bananas?		
Do you like cucumbers?		
Do you like strawberries?		

Fruit and vegetables

35 ☐

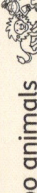

▶ Link.
Verbinde.

tiger Tiger	monkey Affe	elephant Elefant	crocodile Krokodil	zebra Zebra

36

▶ Write in and copy.

Spure nach und schreibe ab.

	a crocodile	
	a monkey	
	a tiger	
	a zebra	
	an elephant	

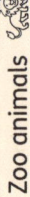
▶ **Read, link and write in.**
Lies, verbinde und spure nach.

Und was kannst du davon?

The elephant can run.

The monkey can jump.

The crocodile can swim.

38

► Which animals do you like? Read and tick.
Welche Tiere magst du? Lies und kreuze an.

Lies immer Frage und Antwort:
Do you like tigers? –
Yes, I do. / No, I don't.

	Yes, I do. ♥	No, I don't.
Do you like tigers?		
Do you like crocodiles?		
Do you like zebras?		
Do you like elephants?		
Do you like monkeys?		

Do you also like giraffes  and lions  ?

▶ Link.
Verbinde.

Traffic

taxi	train	bus	boat	plane
Taxi	Zug	Bus	Boot	Flugzeug

40

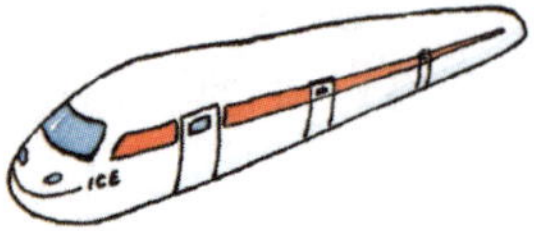

► Read, link and write in.
Lies, verbinde und spure nach.

Lies auch einmal laut.

I go by train.

I go by plane.

I go by boat.

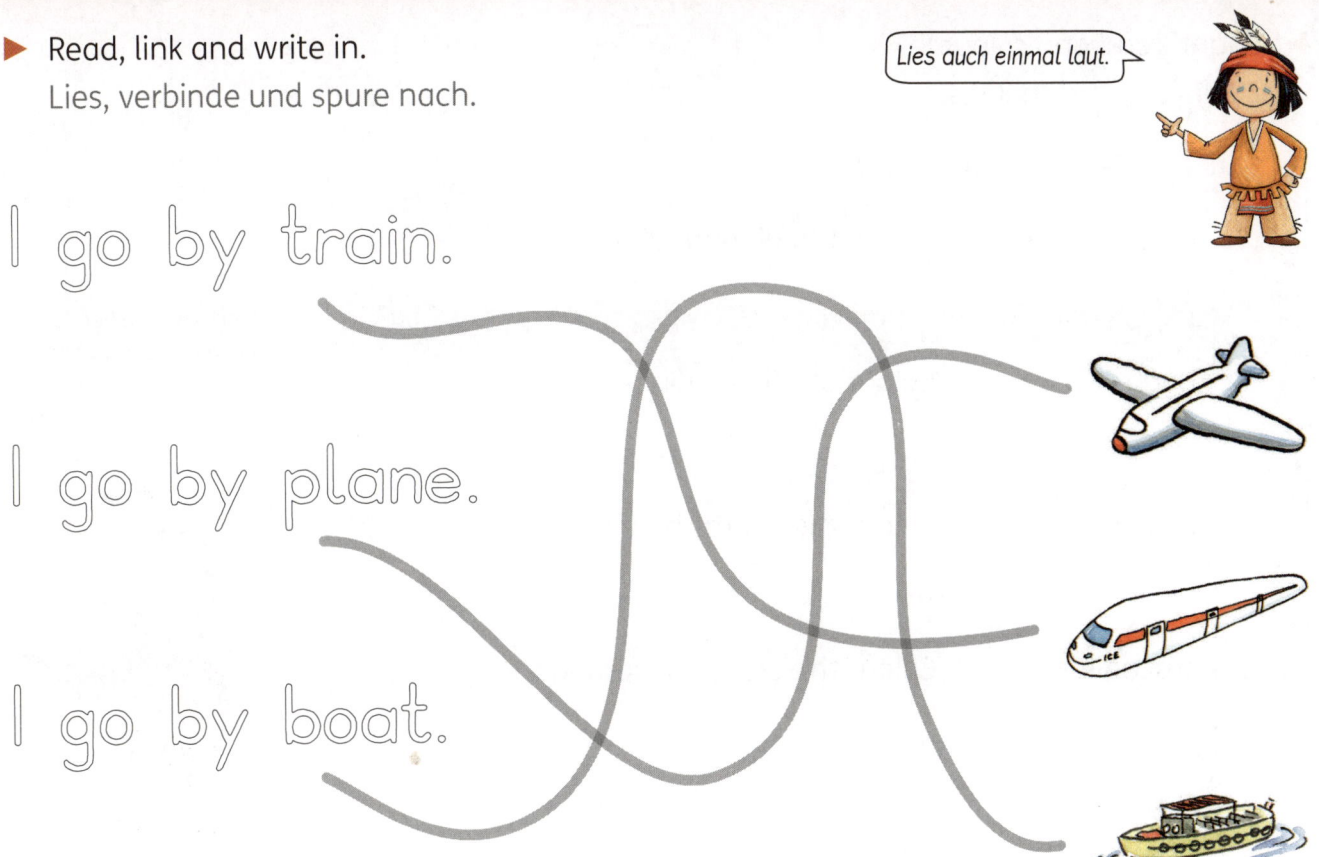

Traffic

▶ Count, read and colour in.
Zähle, lies und male aus.

☐ elephants   Colour the elephants green.

☐ tigers   Colour the tigers white and red.

☐ zebras   Colour the zebras blue and yellow.

☐ crocodiles   Colour the crocodiles orange.

☐ monkeys   Colour the monkeys pink.

Ich bin auch bei der verrückten Safari dabei. Findest du mich?

Crazy safari

School and school uniform

board		die Tafel
chair		der Stuhl
jacket		die Jacke
picture		das Bild
pullover		der Pullover
shirt		das Hemd
skirt		der Rock
table		der Tisch
teacher		der Lehrer, die Lehrerin
trousers		die Hose

Numbers 11 20

eleven	11	elf
twelve	12	zwölf
thirteen	13	dreizehn
forteen	14	vierzehn
fifteen	15	fünfzehn
sixteen	16	sechzehn
seventeen	17	siebzehn
eighteen	18	achtzehn
nineteen	19	neunzehn
twenty	20	zwanzig

Hobbies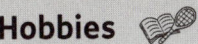

football		Fußball
music		Musik
reading		lesen
skateboarding		Skateboard fahren
swimming		schwimmen

Rooms

bathroom		das Bad
bed		das Bett
bedroom		das Schlafzimmer
chair		der Stuhl
garden		der Garten
kitchen		die Küche
lamp		die Lampe
living room		das Wohnzimmer
shelf		das Regal
table		der Tisch

My words

45

Time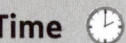

afternoon		der Nachmittag
evening		der Abend
morning		der Morgen
night		die Nacht

Year

autumn		der Herbst
spring		der Frühling
summer		der Sommer
winter		der Winter

Weather

cloudy		wolkig
cold		kalt
hot		heiß
rainy		regnerisch
sunny		sonnig
windy		windig

My words

Fruit and vegetables

apple		der Apfel
banana		die Banane
cucumber		die Gurke
strawberry		die Erdbeere
tomato		die Tomate

Zoo animals

crocodile		das Krokodil
elephant		der Elefant
monkey		der Affe
tiger		der Tiger
zebra		das Zebra

Traffic

bus		der Bus
plane		das Flugzeug
train		der Zug

boat		das Boot, das Schiff
taxi		das Taxi

My words

1. Auflage

1   5   4   3   2   1 | 20   19   18   17   16

Alle Drucke dieser Auflage sind unverändert und können im Unterricht nebeneinander verwendet werden.
Die letzte Zahl bezeichnet das Jahr des Druckes.

Autorin: Antje Maria Greisiger, Leipzig

Redaktion: Antje Maria Greisiger, Leipzig
Herstellung: Gabriele Hager

Layoutkonzeption: know idea gmbh, Freiburg
Illustrationen: Friederike Ablang, Berlin; Yvonne Hoppe-Engbring, Steinfurt; Friederike Schumann, Berlin
Umschlagillustration: Anke Fröhlich, Leipzig
Satz: Kristin Drechsler, Leipzig
Druck: Medienhaus Plump GmbH, Rheinbreitbach

Printed in Germany
ISBN 978-3-12-161053-2